WELCOME TO SPANISH

with SESAME STREET

J. P. PRESS

Lerner Publications ◆ Minneapolis

Dear Parents and Educators,

From its very beginning, *Sesame Street* has promoted mutual respect and cultural understanding by featuring a cast of diverse and lovable characters. *Welcome to Spanish* introduces children to the wonderful, wide world we live in. In this book *Sesame Street* friends present handy and fun vocabulary in a language kids may not know. These words can help young readers welcome new friends. Have fun as you explore!

Sincerely,

The Editors at Sesame Workshop

Table of Contents

WELCOME!

¡Bienvenido!
(Say BYEN-veh-NEE-doh)

4

How to Speak Spanish

Practice speaking Spanish! Each word is broken up into sounds called syllables. Do you see the syllable in CAPITAL LETTERS? That's the sound you emphasize the most!

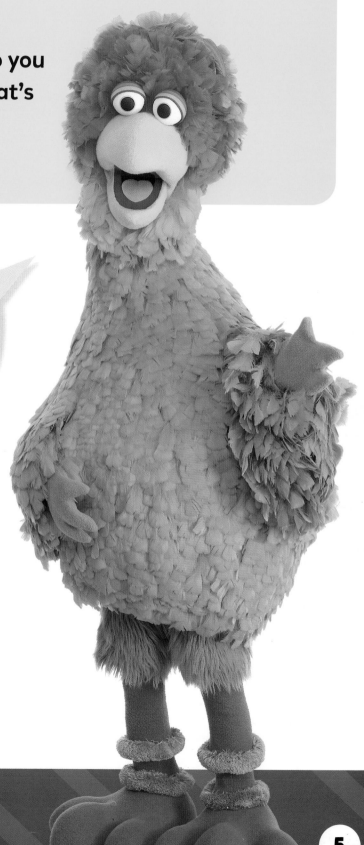

Hello.

Hola.

OH-la

This is Abelardo.
He lives in Mexico.

What is your name?
¿Cómo te llamas?
KOH-moh teh YAH-mahs

My name is . . .
Me llamo . . .
meh YAH-moh . . .

friendship
amistad
ah-mees-tahd

Will you be my friend?
¿Quieres ser mi amigo?
KYEHR-ays sehr
mee ah-MEE-goh

8

Meet my family!

¡Conoce a mi familia!
koh-NOH-say ah mee
fah-MEE-lee-ah

dad
papá
pah-PAH

mom
mamá
mah-MAH

brother
hermano
ehr-MAH-noh

sister
hermana
ehr-MAH-nah

grandma
abuela
ah-BWAY-lah

grandpa
abuelo
ah-BWAY-loh

Thank you.
Gracias.
GRAH-see-ahs

You are welcome.
De nada.
deh NAH-dah

Please.
Por favor.
pore fah-VORE

I'm sorry.
Lo siento.
loh see-EHN-toh

lunch
almuerzo
ahl-MWEHR-soh

breakfast
desayuno
des-ah-YOO-noh

snack
refrigerio
reh-free-HEH-
ree-oh

dinner
cena
SEH-nah

I'm thirsty.
Tengo sed.
TEHN-goh SED

I'm hungry.
Tengo hambre.
TEHN-goh HAHM-bray

Cookie Monster hungry.
Cookie Monster tiene hambre.

15

How are you?

¿Cómo estás?

KOH-moh ehs-TAHS

I'm fine, thank you.

Estoy bien, gracias.

ehs-TOY BYEHN GRAH-see-ahs

I like you.
Me agradas.
meh ah-GRAH-dahs

Elmo loves you.
Elmo te quiere.

happy
contento
cohn-TEN-toh

grumpy
malhumorado
mal-oo-more-ADOH

18

proud

orgulloso

or-goo-YOH-soh

excited

emocionado

eh-moh-see-oh-NAH-doh

animals
animales
ah-nee-MAHL-ehs

dog
perro
PEH-roh

fish
pez
PESS

bird
pájaro
PAH-ha-roh

cat
gato
GAH-toh

I like animals.

Me gustan los animales.

colors
colores
coh-LOH-rehs

My favorite color is . . .
Mi color favorito es . . .
mee cohl-OR
fah-vore-EE-toh
ess . . .

red
rojo
ROH-ho

orange
naranja
nah-RAHN-hah

yellow
amarillo
ah-mah-REE-yoh

green
verde
VEHR-deh

blue
azul
ah-ZOOL

purple
púrpura
POOR-poo-rah

Let's play!
¡Juguemos!
hoo-GAY-mohs

toys
juguetes
hoo-GEH-tehs

What do you like to do?
¿Qué te gusta hacer?
kay teh GOO-stah
ah-SEHR

We love to learn.
Nos encanta aprender.

Goodbye.
Adiós.
ah-DEEOS

See you soon!
¡Hasta pronto!
AH-stah PROHN-toh

Count It!

1 one
uno
OO-noh

2 two
dos
DOHS

3 three
tres
TREHS

4 four
cuatro
KWAH-tro

7 seven
siete
see-EH-teh

5 five
cinco
SEEN-koh

8 eight
ocho
OH-cho

6 six
seis
SAYSS

9 nine
nueve
noo-EH-veh

10 ten
diez
dee-ESS

Rosita's Favorite Words

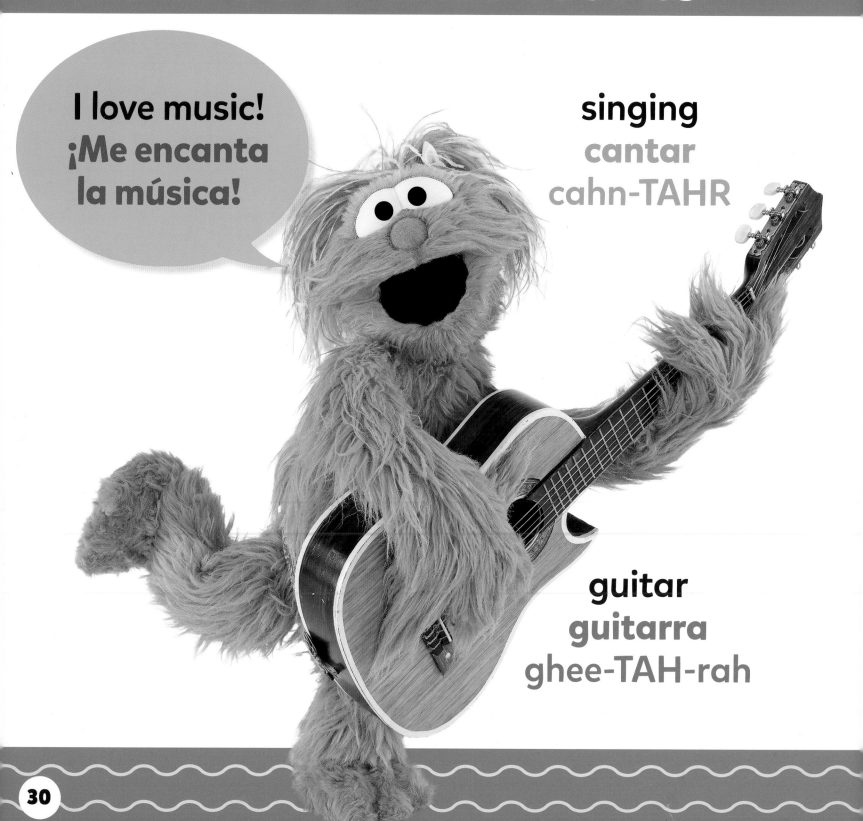

I love music!
¡Me encanta
la música!

singing
cantar
cahn-TAHR

guitar
guitarra
ghee-TAH-rah

Further Information

Atlantic, Leonard. *¡A hacer deportes! / We Play Sports!* New York: Gareth Stevens, 2018.

Graubart, Norman D. *Mi perro / My Dog.* New York: PowerKids, 2014.

Hutchins, J. *Spanish First Words=Primera Palabras en Español.* New York: Scholastic, 2013.

Online Free Spanish: A Fun Way to Learn Spanish
https://onlinefreespanish.com/

PBS Kids: Oh Noah!
http://pbskids.org/noah/index.html

Sesame Street
http://www.sesamestreet.org

Lerner Publications Company
An imprint of Lerner Publishing Group, Inc.
241 First Avenue North
Minneapolis, MN 55401 USA

For reading levels and more information, look up this title at www.lernerbooks.com.

Main body text set in Mikado.
Typeface provided by HVD.

Additional image credits: ESB Professional/Shutterstock.com, p. 20 (dog); clarst5/Shutterstock.com, p. 20 (bird); Eric Isselee/Shutterstock.com, p. 20 (cat); Gunnar Pippel/Shutterstock.com, p. 20 (fish); Super Prin/Shutterstock.com, p. 23 (butterfly).

Library of Congress Cataloging-in-Publication Data

Names: Press, J. P., 1993– author. | Children's Television Workshop, contributor.
Title: Welcome to Spanish with Sesame Street / J. P. Press.
Other titles: Sesame Street (Television program)
Description: Minneapolis : Lerner Publications, 2019. | Series: Sesame Street welcoming words | Includes bibliographical references.
Identifiers: LCCN 2018059331 (print) | LCCN 2019007809 (ebook) | ISBN 9781541562523 (eb pdf) | ISBN 9781541555006 (lb : alk. paper) | ISBN 9781541574977 (pb : alk. paper)
Subjects: LCSH: Spanish language—Conversation and phrase books—English—Juvenile literature.
Classification: LCC PC4121 (ebook) | LCC PC4121 .P74 2019 (print) | DDC 468.2/421—dc23
LC record available at https://lccn.loc.gov/2018059331

Manufactured in the United States of America
1-45825-42702-2/4/2019